ATHENS TRAVEL GUIDE 2024

UNVEILING ATHENS: A JOURNEY THROUGH TIME

SAM OXFORD

Copyright © 2024 by Sam Oxford. All rights reserved.

No part of this book may be reproduced or transmitted in any form or by any means, electronic or mechanical, including photocopying, recording, or by any information storage and retrieval system, without written permission from the author, except for the inclusion of brief quotations in a review.

TABLE OF CONTENTS
1.0 INTRODUCTION TO ATHENS
1.1 WELCOME NOTE
1.2 WHY VISIT ATHENS
1.3 PLANNING YOUR TRIP TO ATHEN

2.1 ARRIVING BY AIR
2.2 ARRIVING BY SEA
2.3 ARRIVING BY LAND

3. ACCOMMODATION
3.1 HOTELS IN ATHENS
3.2 HOSTELS AND BUDGET ACCOMMODATION
3.3 VACATION RENTALS
3.4 CAMPING OPTIONS

4. NAVIGATING ATHENS
4.1 PUBLIC TRANSPORTATION SYSTEM
4.2 WALKING AND BIKING
4.3 TAXIS AND RIDE-SHARING
4.4 CAR RENTALS

5. SIGHTSEEING AND LANDMARKS
5.1 THE ACROPOLIS
5.2 THE PARTHENON
5.3 ANCIENT AGORA
5.4 NATIONAL ARCHAEOLOGICAL MUSEUM
5.5 PLAKA NEIGHBORHOOD
5.6 MONASTIRAKI FLEA MARKET
5.7 SYNTAGMA SQUARE

6. MUSEUMS AND ART GALLERIES
6.1 ACROPOLIS MUSEUM
6.2 BENAKI MUSEUM
6.3 NATIONAL GALLERY
6.4 MUSEUM OF CYCLADIC ART
6.5 WAR MUSEUM
6.6 CONTEMPORARY ART SPACES

7. CULTURAL EXPERIENCES
7.1 GREEK MUSIC AND DANCE
7.2 ATTENDING A GREEK PLAY
7.3 TRADITIONAL FESTIVALS AND EVENTS:

8. SHOPPING IN ATHENS
8.1 SOUVENIR SHOPS:
8.2 FASHION BOUTIQUES:
8.3 LOCAL MARKETS
8.4 ANTIQUE SHOPS:
8.5 JEWELRY STORES:

9. DINING AND CULINARY ADVENTURES
9.1 GREEK CUISINE OVERVIEW:
9.2 BEST RESTAURANTS IN ATHENS:
9.4 VEGETARIAN AND VEGAN OPTIONS:
9.5 DINING ETIQUETTE

10. NIGHTLIFE AND ENTERTAINMENT
10.1 BARS AND NIGHTCLUBS
10.3 THEATERS AND PERFORMING ARTS
10.4 CULTURAL NIGHTLIFE EXPERIENCES

11. DAY TRIPS FROM ATHENS

11.1 CAPE SOUNION AND THE TEMPLE OF POSEIDON
11.2 DELPHI
11.3 EPIDAURUS AND MYCENAE
11.4 HYDRA, POROS, AND AEGINA ISLANDS:
11.5 METEORA MONASTERIES

12. OUTDOOR ACTIVITIES
12.1 BEACHES AND WATER SPORTS
12.2 HIKING AND NATURE TRAILS
12.3 CYCLING ROUTES:
12.4 PARKS AND GARDENS:
12.5 HORSEBACK RIDING:

13. PRACTICAL INFORMATION
13.1 LANGUAGE AND COMMUNICATION
13.2 CURRENCY AND BANKING:
13.3 SAFETY TIPS:
13.4 LOCAL ETIQUETTE:
13.5 EMERGENCY CONTACTS:

14. TRAVEL TIPS
14.1 PACKING LIST:

14.2 BEST TIMES TO VISIT:
14.3 BUDGETING AND COSTS
14.4 VISA AND ENTRY REQUIREMENTS:
14.5 USEFUL APPS AND RESOURCES:

15.0 CONCLUSION
15.1 SUMMARY OF KEY POINTS:
15.2 FINAL THOUGHTS:

1.0 INTRODUCTION TO ATHENS

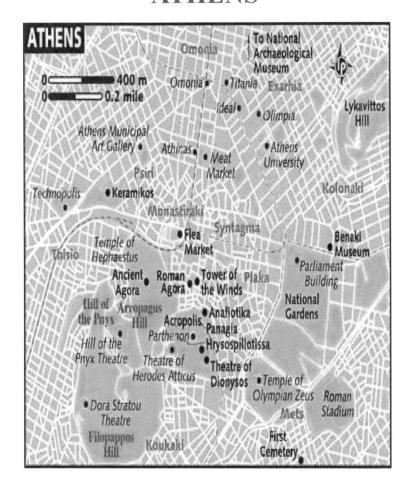

1.1 WELCOME NOTE

Dear Traveler,

With great excitement and warmest greetings, we extend our heartfelt welcome as you embark on a journey to the captivating city of Athens! Nestled amidst the sun-kissed shores of the Aegean Sea, Athens stands as a testament to the rich tapestry of human history and ingenuity.

As you step foot in this remarkable city, prepare to be enchanted by the whispers of ancient legends echoing through the time-worn stones of the Acropolis. Imagine walking in the footsteps of philosophers, poets, and warriors who once graced this land, and let the aura of wisdom and valor embrace your senses.

Athens isn't merely a destination; it's a vibrant mosaic where the past seamlessly intertwines with the present. Marvel at the majesty of the

Parthenon, an architectural masterpiece that has stood the test of millennia, and let its grandeur inspire your imagination. Wander through the narrow alleys of Plaka, where every cobblestone has a story to tell, and lose yourself in the labyrinthine charm of this ancient neighborhood.

Parthenon

But Athens is more than just historical landmarks; it's a city pulsating with life and creativity. Indulge your taste buds in the culinary delights of Greece, savoring olives, feta, and moussaka in cozy tavernas. Dive into the bustling markets of Monastiraki, where vibrant

colors, fragrant spices, and handmade treasures await your discovery. Experience the warmth of Greek hospitality in local cafes, where lively conversations and laughter are the soundtrack of your journey.

Monastiraki market

Venture beyond the city limits, and you'll find idyllic beaches caressed by crystal-clear waters, and sunsets that paint the sky in hues of orange and gold. Explore the nearby islands, each with its unique character, offering an escape into the serene embrace of the Aegean.

As you traverse Athens, let the spirit of this city seep into your soul. Embrace the passion of its people, the richness of its culture, and the timelessness of its heritage. Athens isn't just a destination; it's an experience that will stay with you long after you leave.

We invite you to open your heart to the wonders of Athens, to embrace its ancient charm and modern marvels. Let every moment here be a chapter in your own epic tale, a story you'll share with friends and family, and cherish for a lifetime.

Welcome to Athens, where history, beauty, and hospitality converge to create an unforgettable adventure. May your journey be filled with discovery, joy, and memories that will last a lifetime.

Yours warmly,

Sam Oxford

1.2 WHY VISIT ATHENS

There are countless reasons to visit Athens, the capital city of Greece, and each one offers a unique and compelling experience for travelers. Here's an extensive exploration of why you should consider Athens as your next travel destination:

1. Historical Marvels:

Athens is a city steeped in history. It's the birthplace of democracy and philosophy, making it a pilgrimage site for scholars and history enthusiasts. The iconic Acropolis, an ancient citadel perched atop a rocky outcrop, is a UNESCO World Heritage site and home to several ancient buildings of great architectural and historic significance, including the Parthenon, Erechtheion, and the Temple of Athena Nike. Exploring these ancient marvels provides an unparalleled glimpse into the foundations of Western civilization.

2. Cultural Riches:

Athens boasts a vibrant cultural scene. The city is home to numerous museums, art galleries, theaters, and music venues. The Acropolis Museum, for instance, showcases artifacts from the Acropolis archaeological site, offering an immersive experience into ancient Greek history. The city's theaters host both ancient tragedies and modern performances, allowing visitors to appreciate the continuity of Greece's artistic heritage.

3. Epicurean Delights:

Greek cuisine is renowned worldwide, and Athens is the perfect place to indulge in its authentic flavors. From gyro wraps sold at bustling street corners to fine dining experiences in rooftop restaurants overlooking the Acropolis, Athens offers a culinary adventure like no other. Fresh seafood, olive oil, feta cheese, and honey are just a few ingredients that make Greek cuisine a gastronomic delight.

4. Warm Hospitality:

The Greeks are famous for their hospitality, and Athens is no exception. Visitors are often welcomed with open arms, and locals take pride in sharing their culture, traditions, and stories. Engaging with Athenians provides an opportunity to understand the warmth and friendliness that define Greek hospitality.

5. Picturesque Neighborhoods:

Athens is a city of diverse neighborhoods, each with its own character. Plaka, nestled beneath the Acropolis, is a charming maze of neoclassical houses, labyrinthine streets, and vibrant bougainvillea. Monastiraki is a bustling area known for its markets, where you can find everything from souvenirs to antiques. These neighborhoods offer a glimpse into both the historical and modern aspects of Athenian life.

6. Scenic Beauty:

While Athens is a bustling metropolis, it is also surrounded by natural beauty. The Athenian Riviera stretches along the Saronic Gulf, offering beautiful beaches, seaside resorts, and picturesque fishing villages. Just a short drive from the city, visitors can relax on sandy shores and enjoy the tranquility of the Mediterranean Sea.

7. Gateway to Greek Islands:

Athens serves as a gateway to the stunning Greek islands. From the nearby port of Piraeus, travelers can embark on ferry journeys to islands like Santorini, Mykonos, and Crete. These islands are renowned for their breathtaking landscapes, crystal-clear waters, and rich cultural heritage.

8. Fascinating Blend of Old and New:

Athens seamlessly combines its ancient heritage with a modern, dynamic vibe. While historic sites stand proudly amidst the urban landscape, modern art installations, contemporary architecture, and trendy cafes showcase the city's progressive spirit. This blend of old and new creates a unique atmosphere that appeals to a wide range of travelers.

Athens is not just a city; it's a living tapestry of history, culture, and culinary delights. It's a place where the echoes of ancient philosophers mingle with the laughter of modern Athenians, creating an experience that is both enriching and unforgettable. Whether you are a history buff, a food lover, an art enthusiast, or simply a traveler seeking genuine experiences, Athens invites you to embark on a journey of discovery and inspiration.

1.3 PLANNING YOUR TRIP TO ATHEN

Planning a trip to Athens involves careful consideration of various aspects to ensure a smooth and enjoyable experience.

1. Travel Documents and Visa:

- Check your passport's validity. Ensure it's valid for at least six months beyond your planned departure date.

- Verify the visa requirements for your nationality. Apply for a Schengen visa if required, well in advance of your travel dates.

2. Best Time To Visit:

- Athens experiences a Mediterranean climate. The best times to visit are during the spring (April to June) and fall (September to October) when the weather is pleasant, and tourist crowds are manageable.

- Summer (July to August) can be hot and crowded, but it's also the peak tourist season.

3. Budget and Currency:

- Determine your budget for the trip, considering accommodation, transportation, meals, activities, and souvenirs.

- The currency in Greece is Euro (€). Inform your bank about your travel dates to avoid any issues with your credit/debit cards.

4. Accommodation:

- Research and book your accommodation well in advance, especially if you plan to visit during the peak season. Athens offers a wide range of options, including luxury hotels, budget hostels, and vacation rentals. You will get a full explanation in other chapters.

5. Transportation:

- Book your flights to Athens International Airport (ATH) in advance. Compare prices and consider flexible travel dates for better deals.
- Research local transportation options, including public buses, metro, trams, and taxis, to navigate the city conveniently.

6. Itinerary and Sightseeing:

- Plan your itinerary based on your interests. Allocate time for major attractions like the Acropolis, Ancient Agora, and museums.

- Consider guided tours for a deeper understanding of historical sites. Purchase tickets in advance to avoid long queues, especially for popular attractions like the Acropolis.

- Research lesser-known sites and experiences to explore Athens off the beaten path.

7. Cultural Etiquette and Language:

- Familiarize yourself with Greek customs and etiquette. Greeks are generally warm and welcoming; a simple "Kalimera" (Good morning) goes a long way.

- Learn basic Greek phrases to facilitate communication. Locals appreciate tourists who make an effort to speak their language.

8. Travel Insurance:

- Purchase travel insurance that covers medical emergencies, trip cancellations, and other unforeseen events. Check the coverage details and understand the claim process.

9. Packing:

- Pack appropriate clothing based on the season of your visit. Summers are hot, so light, breathable fabrics are essential. Don't forget sunscreen, sunglasses, and a hat.

- Comfortable walking shoes are a must, especially for exploring historical sites with uneven terrain.

10. Health and Safety:

- Check if any vaccinations are required before your trip.

- Research local health facilities and pharmacies in case of emergencies.

- Be aware of common scams and pickpocketing. Stay in well-lit and populated areas, especially at night.

11. Local Cuisine and Dietary Preferences:

- Explore Greek cuisine, including souvlaki, moussaka, tzatziki, and baklava. Be open to trying local delicacies.

- If you have dietary restrictions, research restaurants that cater to your needs. Greeks are accommodating and willing to modify dishes for vegetarians, vegans, or those with food allergies.

12. Cultural Events and Festivals:

- Check the local events calendar for festivals, concerts, and cultural events happening during your visit. Attending such events can provide a deeper understanding of Greek traditions and contemporary culture.

13. Emergency Contacts and Important Numbers:

- Note down emergency numbers, including local police, ambulance, and your country's embassy or consulate in Athens.

Planning your trip to Athens meticulously ensures you make the most of your time in this historically rich city. With proper preparation, you can immerse yourself in the ancient wonders, vibrant culture, and warm hospitality that Athens has to offer. Safe travels and enjoy your Athenian adventure!

2. GETTING TO ATHENS

2.1 ARRIVING BY AIR:

Arriving by air is the most common and convenient way to reach Athens, as the city is served by the Athens International Airport Eleftherios Venizelos (ATH). This modern airport, located approximately 20 kilometers east of the city center, is one of Europe's busiest and most efficient hubs.

International Connectivity:

Athens International Airport is well-connected to major cities worldwide, making it easy for travelers from diverse corners of the globe to reach the Greek capital. Airlines from various countries operate regular flights to and from Athens, ensuring a smooth travel experience.

Airport Facilities:

The airport boasts modern facilities, including duty-free shops, restaurants serving both local and international cuisine, comfortable lounges, and car rental services. Efficient transportation options such as metro, buses, and taxis are readily available for travelers to reach their accommodations in the city center or other parts of Athens.

Public Transport:

The Athens Metro Line 3 (Blue Line) connects the airport to the city center, offering a convenient and cost-effective way for travelers to reach their destinations. Buses and airport shuttles also provide reliable transportation options, ensuring hassle-free transfers.

2.2 ARRIVING BY SEA:

Athens, with its strategic location along the Aegean Sea, welcomes travelers arriving by sea, offering a picturesque introduction to Greece's coastal beauty.

Piraeus Port:

Piraeus, located about 10 kilometers southwest of Athens, is Greece's largest port and a major gateway for ferries and cruise ships. Travelers arriving from the Greek islands or other

Mediterranean destinations often find themselves greeted by the sight of majestic ships docking in Piraeus harbor.

Ferry Services:

Piraeus serves as a hub for ferry services, connecting Athens to various Greek islands such as Santorini, Mykonos, and Crete. These ferries offer not only a mode of transportation but also a scenic journey across the Aegean, allowing travelers to soak in the maritime charm of the region.

Cruise Ships:

Athens is a popular stop for many cruise lines, enabling travelers to combine their maritime adventures with onshore exploration of the city's historical and cultural treasures.

2.3 ARRIVING BY LAND:

Road Networks:

Athens is well-connected to neighboring European countries via an extensive road network. Travelers can enter Greece by land through various border crossings, such as the Promachonas border with Bulgaria or the Kakavia border with Albania. European travelers often opt for road trips, enjoying the scenic routes and the flexibility of exploring multiple destinations on their way to Athens.

Bus Services:

Several international bus companies operate routes to Athens from neighboring countries. Buses provide a budget-friendly option for travelers, connecting Athens with cities in Bulgaria, North Macedonia, and other Balkan countries.

Rail Services:

While rail travel is less common for international travelers due to limited routes, the Athens Central Railway Station (Larissa Station) serves domestic routes and provides an option for travelers within Greece.

Athens' accessibility by air, sea, and land ensures that travelers have a range of options to choose from, catering to various preferences and travel itineraries. Whether arriving by plane, ferry, or road, the journey to Athens is marked by the anticipation of exploring ancient marvels, experiencing warm Greek hospitality, and embarking on a memorable adventure in one of the world's most historically significant cities.

3. ACCOMMODATION

3.1 HOTELS IN ATHENS:

Luxurious Retreats:

Athens is home to a plethora of upscale hotels, some of which are nestled against the Acropolis or offer panoramic views of the historic sites. These 5-star establishments boast lavish amenities, including spa facilities, rooftop bars, gourmet restaurants, and personalized concierge services. Guests can indulge in opulence while immersing themselves in the city's cultural wonders.

Boutique Charms:

The city is adorned with charming boutique hotels, each with its unique character and design.

These boutique establishments often reflect Athens' artistic and historical ambiance, offering personalized services and intimate atmospheres. Visitors can expect stylish interiors, artistic décor, and a blend of modern comforts with a touch of traditional Greek hospitality.

Business and Conferencing:

Athens is a hub for business travelers, and the city's hotels cater to their specific needs. Many hotels offer state-of-the-art conference facilities, high-speed internet, business centers, and proximity to major business districts. These accommodations ensure that corporate guests can seamlessly balance work commitments with the pleasures of exploring Athens.

Family-Friendly Stays:

Numerous hotels in Athens are designed with families in mind, offering spacious rooms, interconnected suites, and amenities tailored for children. Family-friendly hotels often feature swimming pools, kid's clubs, and babysitting services, ensuring a comfortable and enjoyable stay for families traveling with children.

Historical Elegance:

Some hotels in Athens are housed in restored neoclassical buildings or historical landmarks, allowing guests to experience the city's rich heritage firsthand. Staying in these establishments is akin to stepping back in time, surrounded by the charm and elegance of a bygone era.

3.2 HOSTELS AND BUDGET ACCOMMODATION:

Hostels: Athens boasts a vibrant hostel scene, particularly in areas like Psiri and Monastiraki. Hostels offer budget travelers a sociable and affordable accommodation option. Dormitory-style rooms, communal spaces, and organized events create a lively atmosphere where guests can connect with fellow travelers. Hostels often provide essential amenities, such as shared kitchens, lockers, and free Wi-Fi, making them popular among backpackers and solo travelers.

Budget Hotels and Guesthouses: Apart from hostels, Athens has a range of budget hotels, guesthouses, and pensions that provide economical yet comfortable lodgings. These accommodations offer private rooms, ensuring more privacy than dormitory-style hostels. Budget travelers can enjoy the convenience of central locations, allowing easy access to Athens' attractions without breaking the bank.

Apartment Rentals: With the rise of online platforms, renting apartments and vacation homes has become a popular choice for travelers seeking more independence and flexibility. Athens offers a variety of furnished apartments and studios equipped with kitchens, allowing guests to prepare their meals and live like locals. This option is ideal for families, groups, or travelers planning an extended stay in the city.

Athens' accommodation scene caters to a diverse audience, ranging from luxury seekers to budget-conscious explorers. Whether you prefer the opulence of a 5-star hotel, the charm of a boutique establishment, the sociability of a hostel, or the independence of a rented apartment, Athens ensures that your stay is as memorable and enjoyable as your explorations of its ancient marvels and vibrant neighborhoods.

3.3 VACATION RENTALS

Apartments:

Athens boasts a thriving market for vacation apartment rentals. Travelers can choose from a variety of apartments, ranging from cozy studios to spacious penthouses. These rentals often come equipped with modern amenities such as fully equipped kitchens, Wi-Fi, and laundry facilities, providing guests with a home-like experience. Many apartments are strategically located near major attractions, allowing travelers to immerse themselves in the city's vibrant atmosphere.

Villas:

For those seeking luxury and privacy, Athens offers exquisite villas in the outskirts and nearby coastal areas. These villas often come with private pools, lush gardens, and panoramic views of the Aegean Sea. They provide an ideal retreat for families, groups, or couples looking for a tranquil and lavish escape from the city's hustle and bustle.

Historical Homes: Athens is dotted with historic homes that have been lovingly restored and transformed into vacation rentals. Staying in one of these heritage properties offers travelers a unique opportunity to experience the city's architectural legacy. Guests can enjoy the charm of traditional Greek homes, complete with authentic furnishings and décor, providing an immersive cultural experience.

Local Experiences: Vacation rentals allow travelers to connect with locals and experience Athens from a resident's perspective. Many hosts provide personalized recommendations, insider tips, and sometimes even guided tours, ensuring that guests make the most of their Athenian adventure.

3.4 CAMPING OPTIONS:

Camping Sites:

Athens and its surrounding areas offer several camping sites for nature enthusiasts and adventure seekers. These sites provide a budget-friendly accommodation option, allowing travelers to immerse themselves in the region's natural beauty. Many camping sites offer facilities such as tents, caravans, communal kitchens, and bathrooms.

Beachside Camping:

Along the Athenian Riviera, travelers can find beachside campsites that provide a unique coastal camping experience. Waking up to the sound of waves and enjoying sunsets over the sea create unforgettable memories. These sites offer a perfect blend of outdoor living and beach relaxation, making them popular among beach lovers.

Athens' accommodation options extend far beyond traditional hotels, providing travelers with a wide array of choices to suit their preferences and interests. Whether it's the privacy of a villa, the cultural immersion of a historical home, the local insights from a vacation rental, or the adventure of camping in nature, Athens ensures that every visitor finds a home away from home, allowing them to embrace the city's warmth and hospitality while exploring its ancient wonders and contemporary delights.

4. NAVIGATING ATHENS

4.1 PUBLIC TRANSPORTATION SYSTEM:

Athens Metro:

The Athens Metro, consisting of three lines (Green, Red, and Blue), serves as the backbone of the city's public transportation. It connects major attractions, neighborhoods, and the suburbs, making it the fastest and most convenient way to travel. The metro is clean, efficient, and well-connected, allowing travelers to avoid traffic congestion.

Buses and Trolleys:

Athens boasts an extensive bus and trolleybus network that covers areas not reached by the metro. Buses are especially useful for reaching destinations on the outskirts and suburbs. They are an economical option and offer a chance to see the city while traveling. Trolleys, identifiable by their overhead electric lines, follow specific routes and are part of the city's public transport system.

Trams:

The Athens Tram connects the city center with the coastal suburbs, offering a scenic route along the Athenian Riviera. Traveling by tram provides a relaxing way to enjoy beautiful sea views, making it a popular choice for tourists and locals alike.

Suburban Railway (Proastiakos): The Proastiakos suburban railway connects Athens with nearby towns and regions, offering a convenient means of traveling outside the city.

It's particularly useful for day trips to places like Corinth, Chalkida, and the airport.

4.2 WALKING AND BIKING:

Pedestrian-Friendly Areas:

Many areas in Athens, including the historic Plaka district and the bustling Monastiraki square, are pedestrian-friendly. Walking allows travelers to soak in the city's atmosphere, explore charming alleys, and discover hidden gems at their own pace.

Biking Trails:

Athens has been actively promoting cycling as an eco-friendly means of transportation. The city has designated bike lanes and several cycling trails, especially along the Athens Riviera. Travelers can rent bikes and explore coastal routes, combining physical activity with sightseeing.

4.3 TAXIS AND RIDE-SHARING:

Taxis:

Taxis are readily available in Athens and can be hailed on the street or found at designated taxi stands. They are metered, and it's advisable to ensure the meter is on to avoid disputes. Taxis provide a convenient option, especially when traveling with luggage or late at night.

Ride-Sharing Apps:

Ride-sharing services like Uber operate in Athens, offering an alternative to traditional taxis. These apps provide fare estimates, driver details, and a cashless payment system, enhancing convenience for travelers.

4.4 CAR RENTALS:

Renting a Car: While public transportation is robust, renting a car can be advantageous for travelers wanting to explore destinations beyond Athens, such as archaeological sites, beaches, and picturesque villages. Several international and local car rental companies operate in the city, providing a range of vehicles to suit different needs.

Driving Considerations: It's essential to familiarize yourself with Greek traffic rules, road signs, and parking regulations before driving in Athens. Traffic in the city can be hectic, especially during rush hours, so drivers should exercise caution and patience.

Navigating Athens offers a blend of ancient charm and modern convenience. Whether you choose the efficient metro, the scenic tram, the freedom of a rental car, or the leisure of walking or biking, each mode of transportation provides a unique perspective of the city. Athens, with its diverse transportation options, ensures that travelers can explore its historical wonders and contemporary delights with ease and flexibility, making every journey a memorable experience.

5. SIGHTSEEING AND LANDMARKS

5.1 THE ACROPOLIS:

Iconic Citadel:

The Acropolis of Athens, a UNESCO World Heritage Site, stands proudly as the symbol of ancient Greece's architectural and artistic achievements. This monumental citadel, perched atop a rocky outcrop, overlooks the city, offering breathtaking panoramic views.

Parade of Temples:

The Acropolis complex houses several awe-inspiring structures, the most notable of which is the Parthenon, a temple dedicated to the goddess Athena. The Parthenon's Doric columns, intricate friezes, and architectural precision showcase the pinnacle of classical Greek architecture.

Erechtheion:

Adjacent to the Parthenon, the Erechtheion is another significant temple on the Acropolis. It is renowned for its Caryatids, sculpted female figures serving as columns, adding an elegant touch to the structure.

Propylaea and Temple of Athena Nike:

The Propylaea, the grand entrance to the Acropolis, and the Temple of Athena Nike, dedicated to the goddess of victory, complete the ensemble of ancient marvels on this sacred hill.

5.2 THE PARTHENON:

Architectural Marvel: The Parthenon, an enduring symbol of ancient Greece's cultural and artistic prowess, is a temple dedicated to the goddess Athena, the city's patron deity. Its design, characterized by Doric columns and intricate friezes, reflects the ideals of classical Greek architecture.

Cultural Significance: Beyond its architectural magnificence, the Parthenon embodies the essence of Athenian democracy, philosophy, and artistic expression. It stands as a testament to the city's intellectual and cultural achievements during the Golden Age of Athens.

Restoration Efforts: Over centuries, the Parthenon has undergone various transformations and faced natural disasters. Extensive restoration work is ongoing, preserving its grandeur and ensuring that future generations can marvel at this ancient wonder.

5.3 ANCIENT AGORA:

Historical Marketplace: The Ancient Agora served as the heart of ancient Athens, functioning as a marketplace, political hub, and social center. It was a bustling area where merchants, philosophers, and citizens congregated, shaping the city's cultural and political landscape.

Temple of Hephaestus:

Dominating the Ancient Agora, the Temple of Hephaestus, dedicated to the god of craftsmanship, is one of the best-preserved ancient Greek temples. Its Doric columns and intricate friezes exemplify classical Greek architecture at its finest.

Stoa of Attalos:

The Stoa of Attalos, a reconstructed colonnade, now houses the Museum of the Ancient Agora. The museum showcases artifacts from ancient Athens, offering visitors a glimpse into daily life, art, and governance in antiquity.

Visiting these landmarks in Athens is like stepping back in time, immersing yourself in the legacy of ancient Greece. Each site tells a story of innovation, democracy, and artistic brilliance, making Athens a destination where history comes to life, captivating the imagination of every visitor.

5.4 NATIONAL ARCHAEOLOGICAL MUSEUM

Treasure Trove of Antiquities: The National Archaeological Museum in Athens is one of the world's great museums, housing an astounding collection of artifacts from ancient Greece. Its exhibits span thousands of years, showcasing sculptures, pottery, jewelry, and art from various periods, including the Minoan, Mycenaean, and Classical eras.

Showcase of Greek Civilization: The museum's exhibits offer a comprehensive overview of Greek civilization, highlighting the artistic achievements, religious practices, and everyday life of ancient Greeks. Notable displays include the Mask of Agamemnon, the Antikythera Mechanism, and the Artemision Bronze.

Educational Experience: The museum provides a rich educational experience, allowing visitors to delve deep into the history and mythology of Greece. Its well-curated displays and informative signage make it a must-visit for history enthusiasts and anyone interested in ancient cultures.

5.5 PLAKA NEIGHBORHOOD:

Historical Charm: Plaka, nestled at the foot of the Acropolis, is one of Athens' oldest and most picturesque neighborhoods. Its narrow cobblestone streets, neoclassical buildings, and vibrant bougainvillea create a charming atmosphere that transports visitors to a bygone era.

Tavernas and Cafés: Plaka is dotted with traditional tavernas, cozy cafés, and ouzeries, where visitors can savor authentic Greek cuisine and local delicacies. Dining in Plaka offers not just a meal but a cultural experience, with the ambiance enhanced by live music and warm hospitality.

Shopping and Souvenirs:

Plaka is a shopper's paradise, offering a wide range of boutiques, souvenir shops, and artisanal stores. Visitors can find unique items such as handmade crafts, jewelry, olive products, and Greek textiles, making it an ideal place to buy souvenirs and gifts.

5.6 MONASTIRAKI FLEA MARKET:

Treasure Hunt: The Monastiraki Flea Market, located near the Acropolis and Plaka, is a vibrant maze of stalls selling everything from vintage clothing and antiques to handmade crafts and artwork. Exploring the market feels like a treasure hunt, with unexpected finds waiting at every corner.

Eclectic Atmosphere: The market's eclectic atmosphere, infused with the scent of spices, the sound of street musicians, and the vibrant colors of goods on display, creates a sensory delight for visitors. It's a place where the old and the new coexist, offering a glimpse into Athens' diverse cultural tapestry.

Bargaining and Interaction: Bargaining is a common practice at the Monastiraki Flea Market, allowing visitors to engage in friendly negotiations with vendors. This interactive experience adds to the market's charm, creating a lively and dynamic atmosphere.

5.7 SYNTAGMA SQUARE:

Political Center: Syntagma Square is the political heart of Athens, housing the Hellenic Parliament and the Tomb of the Unknown Soldier. The square is not only a site of historical significance but also a hub of civic activities, including protests, celebrations, and cultural events.

Luxury and Elegance: Surrounding Syntagma Square, visitors can find luxury hotels, high-end boutiques, and gourmet restaurants. The area exudes an air of elegance, making it a popular destination for upscale shopping and dining experiences.

Changing of the Guard: One of the notable attractions at Syntagma Square is the changing of the guard ceremony at the Tomb of the Unknown Soldier. The Evzones, members of the Presidential Guard, dressed in traditional attire, perform this ceremonial duty with precision and solemnity, attracting crowds of spectators.

Athens offers a multifaceted experience that goes beyond its ancient ruins. From exploring world-class museums like the National Archaeological Museum to wandering through the charming streets of Plaka and indulging in the vibrant atmosphere of Monastiraki Flea Market, and witnessing the historical and political significance of Syntagma Square, visitors can delve into the diverse and dynamic soul of the city. These attractions add layers to Athens' narrative, creating a travel experience that combines historical depth with contemporary vitality.

6. MUSEUMS AND ART GALLERIES

Athens, a city steeped in antiquity, is also a hub of artistic and cultural expression. Its museums and art galleries serve as windows into the rich tapestry of Greek history, art, and creativity. Here's an extensive guide to some of the prominent museums and galleries in Athens:

6.1 ACROPOLIS MUSEUM:

Architectural Marvel:

The Acropolis Museum, located at the foot of the Acropolis itself, is a masterpiece of modern architecture. Its design, characterized by glass floors showcasing ancient ruins, provides a unique juxtaposition of the contemporary and the ancient.

Custodian of Antiquities:

The museum houses artifacts from the Acropolis archaeological site, including sculptures, pottery, and architectural fragments. The focal point is the Gallery of the Parthenon Marbles, displaying the renowned sculptures from the Parthenon, offering visitors a close encounter with the masterpieces of classical Greek art.

Historical Context:

The museum not only showcases the artifacts but also provides historical context through multimedia exhibits and detailed explanations. Visitors can gain a deep understanding of the religious, cultural, and artistic significance of the Acropolis and its sculptures.

Panoramic Views:

The museum's top-floor terrace offers panoramic views of the Acropolis, creating a serene atmosphere where visitors can reflect on the

historical significance of the site while enjoying breathtaking vistas of the ancient citadel.

6.2 BENAKI MUSEUM:

Cultural Odyssey:

The Benaki Museum is a cultural odyssey through Greek history, featuring a diverse collection of artifacts from various periods, including prehistoric, Byzantine, and Ottoman eras. Its exhibits provide a comprehensive overview of Greece's historical and cultural evolution.

Artistic Treasures:
In addition to historical artifacts, the Benaki Museum houses a remarkable collection of Greek artworks, including paintings, sculptures, and decorative arts. The museum's emphasis on artistic expression offers visitors a glimpse into Greece's creative legacy.

Specialized Collections: The Benaki Museum boasts specialized collections, such as the Museum of Islamic Art, showcasing Islamic art and artifacts, and the Nikos Hadjikyriakos-Ghika Gallery, dedicated to the works of the renowned Greek artist.

6.3 NATIONAL GALLERY:

Greek Art Through the Ages:

The National Gallery is Greece's foremost art museum, displaying a rich collection of Greek art from the 19th century to the present day. Its exhibits feature the works of prominent Greek artists, reflecting the country's artistic evolution over the centuries.

Landscapes and Portraits:

The museum's galleries showcase a wide array of artworks, including landscapes depicting Greece's natural beauty and portraits capturing the essence of Greek figures. Visitors can explore the evolution of artistic styles, from traditional realism to modern and abstract expressions.

Temporary Exhibitions:

In addition to its permanent collection, the National Gallery hosts temporary exhibitions, featuring contemporary artists and thematic displays. These exhibitions provide insights into current trends and artistic innovations within the Greek art scene.

Educational Programs:

The National Gallery offers educational programs, workshops, and guided tours, making it an engaging destination for art enthusiasts, students, and families. These initiatives promote art appreciation and cultural understanding among visitors of all ages.

Athens' museums and art galleries offer immersive journeys through time, artistry, and culture. From the architectural splendor of the Acropolis Museum to the diverse collections of the Benaki Museum and the National Gallery, these institutions celebrate Greece's rich heritage and creative spirit. Whether you're a history buff, an art aficionado, or a curious traveler, Athens' museums and galleries provide enriching experiences that deepen your understanding of Greek art, history, and cultural identity.

6.4 MUSEUM OF CYCLADIC ART

Ancient Elegance: The Museum of Cycladic Art is a testament to the elegance of ancient Greek art. Focused primarily on the Cycladic civilization, the museum displays marble figurines, pottery, and artifacts from the Cycladic islands, offering a glimpse into the artistic achievements of this enigmatic civilization.

Intriguing Exhibits: The museum's exhibits explore the art and culture of the Cycladic people, renowned for their minimalist and abstract sculptures. Visitors can marvel at the intricate craftsmanship of ancient artifacts, gaining insights into the Cycladic way of life and artistic sensibilities.

Cultural Context: The Museum of Cycladic Art places these artifacts within their historical and cultural context, shedding light on the religious beliefs, burial practices, and artistic traditions of the Cycladic civilization. The museum's thematic exhibits provide a comprehensive understanding of this ancient culture.

6.5 WAR MUSEUM:

Military Heritage: The War Museum of Athens pays homage to Greece's military heritage, chronicling the country's history of warfare and the heroic struggles of its people. The museum showcases artifacts, uniforms, weapons, and documents from various periods, including the Greek War of Independence and both World Wars.

Interactive Exhibits: The museum offers interactive exhibits, multimedia presentations, and dioramas that bring historical events to life. Visitors can gain a deep understanding of

Greece's wartime experiences, the evolution of military technology, and the sacrifices made by soldiers and civilians alike.

Memorial Garden: The War Museum features a memorial garden adorned with military equipment, aircraft, and artillery pieces. This outdoor exhibit allows visitors to explore military vehicles and aircraft, providing a hands-on experience of Greece's military history.

6.6 CONTEMPORARY ART SPACES

EMST– National Museum of Contemporary Art

EMST is Greece's flagship museum dedicated to contemporary art. Housed in the former Fix brewery, the museum showcases a vast collection of Greek and international contemporary artworks, including paintings, sculptures, installations, and multimedia pieces. It serves as a platform for innovative and experimental artistic expressions, reflecting the dynamic nature of contemporary art.

Benaki Museum Pireos Annex:

The Benaki Museum's Pireos Annex is a hub of contemporary creativity, hosting temporary exhibitions, performances, and cultural events. It features works by emerging and established artists, fostering dialogues around contemporary social, political, and cultural themes. The museum's diverse exhibits provide visitors with a glimpse into the evolving landscape of contemporary Greek art.

Art Spaces and Galleries:

Athens is dotted with independent art spaces, galleries, and artist-run initiatives. Areas like Exarchia and Metaxourgeio are known for their alternative art scenes, hosting exhibitions, performances, and workshops by local and international artists. These spaces offer a platform for experimental and boundary-pushing art, showcasing the city's avant-garde spirit.

Athens' museums and contemporary art spaces offer a multifaceted exploration of artistic expression, spanning ancient civilizations, military history, and cutting-edge contemporary art. Whether you're drawn to the mystery of ancient Cycladic art, the heroism of wartime struggles, or the innovative visions of contemporary artists, Athens provides a rich tapestry of cultural experiences, inviting visitors to delve into the diverse and evolving world of art and creativity.

7. CULTURAL EXPERIENCES

7.1 GREEK MUSIC AND DANCE:

Traditional Music:

Greek music is as diverse as the country's landscapes. Traditional music genres like rebetiko, with its soulful melodies and poignant lyrics, capture the essence of Greek folk heritage. Rebetiko, often performed in intimate settings, conveys themes of love, loss, and resilience, resonating deeply with listeners.

Bouzouki Sounds:

The bouzouki, a stringed musical instrument, is synonymous with Greek music. Its lively tunes and spirited rhythms evoke a sense of celebration and camaraderie. Visitors can enjoy live bouzouki performances in traditional tavernas and music venues, immersing themselves in the vivacious sounds of Greece.

Greek Folk Dance:

Greek folk dances, such as syrtaki and zeibekiko, are an integral part of Greek culture. These dances, often performed at celebrations and festivals, reflect the country's regional diversity and historical narratives. Participating in these dances, guided by skilled dancers, offers a firsthand experience of Athenian exuberance and joie de vivre.

Cultural Festivals: Athens hosts various cultural festivals throughout the year, showcasing Greek music, dance, and performing arts. The Athens Epidaurus Festival, held in ancient theaters, features world-class performances, bringing together artists from Greece and abroad. These festivals create a vibrant atmosphere, allowing visitors to immerse themselves in the city's cultural vibrancy.

Athens' cultural experiences, rooted in the traditions of Greek cuisine and music, offer travelers a sensory and immersive journey. Whether savoring the flavors of mezedes in a lively taverna, dancing to the rhythms of bouzouki music, or exploring the city's food markets, every encounter in Athens is an opportunity to connect with the city's rich cultural heritage and experience the warmth of Greek hospitality.

7.2 ATTENDING A GREEK PLAY

Theater of Dionysus:

At the Theater of Dionysus, located at the foot of the Acropolis, visitors can witness the magic of ancient Greek drama. Imagine sitting on stone seats, surrounded by ancient ruins, as timeless plays by playwrights like Aeschylus, Sophocles, and Euripides come to life. The theater's acoustics and atmosphere enhance the experience, transporting audiences to the days of classical Athens.

Epidaurus Theater:

For an even more enchanting experience, attending a play at the Epidaurus Theater is a must. This ancient theater, renowned for its impeccable acoustics, offers an unparalleled setting for Greek tragedies and comedies. The sound of actors' voices carries effortlessly to every corner, creating an immersive theatrical experience that resonates with the spirit of ancient drama.

Summer Festivals:

Athens hosts summer festivals, such as the Athens Epidaurus Festival, where both ancient and contemporary plays are performed in historic theaters. The blend of ancient architecture and modern interpretations creates a dynamic and unforgettable experience for theater enthusiasts.

7.3 TRADITIONAL FESTIVALS AND EVENTS:

Easter Celebrations:

Easter is a significant cultural and religious celebration in Greece. Athens comes alive with festivities, including religious processions, church services, and feasts. Visitors can witness the spectacular midnight Resurrection service at churches like the Metropolitan Cathedral, followed by traditional feasts featuring delicacies like lamb, tsoureki (Easter bread), and red-dyed eggs.

Apokries (Carnival):

Apokries, the Greek carnival season, is celebrated with colorful parades, masquerade parties, and lively music and dance. The heart of the carnival festivities is in neighborhoods like Plaka and Psiri, where locals and visitors don costumes and join the revelry. Traditional music, dance, and street performances create a festive ambiance, making it a joyous time to experience Athenian culture.

Panigiri (Folk Festivals):

Throughout the year, Athens hosts panigiri, traditional folk festivals celebrated in honor of saints. These festivals feature live music, traditional dances, and local delicacies. Locals and tourists alike gather in neighborhoods like Monastiraki and Thisio to partake in the festivities, creating a communal atmosphere infused with Greek hospitality.

Ochi Day:

Ochi Day, celebrated on October 28th, commemorates Greece's refusal to surrender to the Axis powers during World War II. The day is marked by military parades, school performances, and patriotic events. Syntagma Square and other central locations host grand celebrations, providing a glimpse into Greece's historical pride and resilience.

Athens' cultural experiences, from attending ancient Greek plays in historic theaters to participating in lively traditional festivals, offer travelers a profound connection to the city's rich heritage. These events and traditions provide an opportunity to witness the enduring spirit of Greek culture, fostering a sense of camaraderie and celebration that lingers in the hearts of all who experience them.

8. SHOPPING IN ATHENS

8.1 SOUVENIR SHOPS:

Monastiraki Flea Market:

Monastiraki, located at the heart of Athens, is a bustling area known for its vibrant flea market. Here, you can find an array of souvenirs, including traditional Greek pottery, handmade jewelry, leather goods, and iconic evil eye charms. The narrow alleys are filled with small shops and stalls, creating a maze of discoveries for souvenir hunters.

Plaka District:

Plaka, one of the oldest neighborhoods in Athens, is a treasure trove of souvenir shops. Wandering through its winding streets, visitors encounter shops selling items like Greek spices, olive oil products, local wines, and decorative items inspired by ancient Greek art. Plaka's quaint boutiques offer an authentic Athenian shopping experience.

Ermou Street:

Ermou Street, a bustling shopping avenue in central Athens, features a mix of international brands and souvenir shops. Here, you can find a variety of Greek-themed souvenirs, from T-shirts and magnets to traditional musical instruments and replicas of ancient artifacts. Ermou Street is a convenient destination for travelers looking to shop for souvenirs alongside popular fashion brands.

8.2 FASHION BOUTIQUES:

Kolonaki District:

Known as Athens' upscale shopping district, Kolonaki is home to luxurious boutiques and designer stores. Fashion enthusiasts can explore high-end brands, Greek and international alike, offering everything from clothing and accessories to cosmetics and jewelry. Kolonaki's stylish atmosphere and exclusive shops make it a haven for fashion connoisseurs.

Eolou Street: Eolou Street, located near Monastiraki, is a hub for independent fashion boutiques and concept stores. Here, you can discover unique clothing pieces, handmade accessories, and contemporary designs by local designers. Eolou Street is a paradise for fashion lovers seeking one-of-a-kind items that reflect Athens' modern style.

The Mall Athens:

For a comprehensive shopping experience, The Mall Athens, located in the Marousi suburb, offers a vast selection of Greek and international brands. From fashion and electronics to home decor and beauty products, the mall caters to diverse shopping preferences. It also features entertainment options, restaurants, and cafes, making it a destination for a day of shopping and leisure.

Voukourestiou Street:

Voukourestiou Street, nestled in the heart of Athens, is renowned for its upscale boutiques and fine jewelry stores. Here, you can find renowned Greek and international designers, showcasing exquisite clothing, accessories, and jewelry pieces. The street's elegant ambiance and sophisticated offerings attract fashion enthusiasts seeking luxury and refinement.

Shopping in Athens is a delightful blend of tradition and modernity, offering an array of options for souvenir hunters and fashion enthusiasts alike. Whether you're exploring the vibrant markets of Monastiraki, indulging in luxury brands in Kolonaki, or discovering unique designs in independent boutiques, Athens' shopping destinations cater to diverse tastes, making every shopping excursion a memorable experience.

8.3 LOCAL MARKETS

Varvakios Agora:

Varvakios Agora, Athens' central food market, is a sensory delight. Located near Monastiraki, it's a bustling hub of activity where locals and visitors alike come to shop for fresh fruits, vegetables, meat, fish, spices, and more. The vibrant atmosphere, aromatic scents, and colorful displays create a captivating experience. Visitors can interact with friendly vendors, sample local products, and witness the lively essence of Athenian daily life.

Athens Central Market:

The Athens Central Market, also known as the Dimotiki Agora, is another local market offering a wide array of fresh produce, meats, cheeses, and spices. The market's historic building adds to its charm, and exploring the stalls gives visitors a glimpse into traditional Greek gastronomy. The market is an excellent place to immerse yourself in the city's culinary culture and purchase high-quality local ingredients.

8.4 ANTIQUE SHOPS:

Dionysiou Areopagitou Street: This picturesque street near the Acropolis is lined with antique shops offering a captivating selection of vintage items, artifacts, and collectibles. Antique enthusiasts can find everything from furniture and ceramics to old books and artwork. Exploring these shops feels like a journey through time, where each item has a story to tell, making it a paradise for history lovers and collectors.

Athens Antiques Market: The Athens Antiques Market, located in the Monastiraki area, is a treasure trove for antique lovers. The market features a variety of antique shops and stalls selling a diverse range of items, including furniture, jewelry, coins, and vintage clothing. Bargaining is common here, allowing visitors to strike good deals while discovering unique pieces from different eras.

8.5 JEWELRY STORES:

Plaka Jewelry Shops: The historic Plaka district is home to numerous jewelry stores offering a wide selection of items, from traditional Greek designs to contemporary pieces. Visitors can find handmade jewelry crafted with semi-precious stones, gold, and silver. These shops often showcase intricate filigree work, inspired by ancient Greek motifs, allowing buyers to take home beautifully crafted souvenirs or luxurious gifts.

Ermou Street Jewelry Boutiques: Ermou Street, Athens' main shopping avenue, hosts a range of jewelry boutiques representing both local and international brands. Here, visitors can explore modern and stylish jewelry collections, from elegant diamond pieces to trendy accessories. These boutiques provide a luxurious shopping experience, allowing buyers to indulge in high-quality jewelry crafted with exquisite precision.

Greek Orthodox Jewelry Stores: Athens is known for its unique Greek Orthodox religious jewelry, including icons, crosses, and religious charms. Visitors can find specialized stores around Monastiraki and Syntagma Square that offer a variety of religious artifacts and jewelry items, providing insight into Greece's religious and cultural heritage.

Athens' shopping experiences, whether exploring bustling local markets, discovering antique treasures, or indulging in the elegance of jewelry boutiques, offer a captivating blend of tradition, artistry, and history. Each shopping excursion in Athens is a cultural adventure, providing opportunities to connect with the city's heritage and take home cherished mementos of your journey.

9. DINING AND CULINARY ADVENTURES

9.1 GREEK CUISINE OVERVIEW:

Mediterranean Bounty:

Greek cuisine is a celebration of fresh, high-quality ingredients. With its foundation in the Mediterranean diet, it emphasizes olive oil, grains, vegetables, and seafood. Herbs like oregano, thyme, and rosemary add depth to the flavors, while feta cheese, olives, and yogurt are staples in many dishes.

Mezedes and Sharing Culture:

Mezedes, a variety of small, flavorful dishes, are an integral part of Greek dining. Spanakopita (spinach pie), moussaka (layered eggplant dish), tzatziki (yogurt and cucumber dip), and souvlaki (grilled meat skewers) are just a few examples. Greeks enjoy these dishes in a communal setting, fostering a sense of camaraderie and connection.

Fresh Seafood:

Athens' proximity to the Aegean Sea ensures an abundance of fresh seafood. From grilled octopus and succulent fish to seafood pasta and fried calamari, Athenian restaurants offer a wide selection of delectable seafood dishes that capture the essence of coastal Greek cuisine.

Desserts and Pastries:

Greek desserts are a delightful indulgence. Baklava, layers of filo pastry with nuts and honey, is a beloved treat. Loukoumades, deep-fried dough balls drizzled with honey and cinnamon, offer a sweet and crispy experience. Additionally, Greek yogurt served with honey and nuts is a popular and healthy dessert option.

9.2 BEST RESTAURANTS IN ATHENS:

To Kafeneio:

This traditional taverna in Plaka offers an authentic Greek dining experience. With its rustic charm and warm ambiance, To Kafeneio serves classic dishes prepared with fresh, locally sourced ingredients. Guests can savor grilled meats, mezedes, and seafood while enjoying live music performances.

Ta Karamanlidika Tou Fani:

This unique deli and restaurant in Monastiraki specializes in cured meats, cheeses, and traditional Greek flavors. The menu features an array of mezedes, homemade sausages, and artisanal cheeses. Guests can enjoy a selection of gourmet dishes, showcasing the best of Greek charcuterie and culinary craftsmanship.

Aleria Restaurant:

Aleria, located in the Metaxourgeio neighborhood, offers a modern twist on Greek cuisine. The menu combines traditional recipes with innovative techniques, resulting in dishes that are both familiar and inventive. The restaurant's stylish décor and creative culinary creations make it a favorite among food enthusiasts seeking a contemporary dining experience.

Varoulko Seaside:

For seafood aficionados, Varoulko Seaside, situated near the Mikrolimano Marina, is a culinary gem. Led by acclaimed chef Lefteris Lazarou, the restaurant specializes in exquisite seafood dishes prepared with artistic flair. The menu showcases the freshest catch of the day, expertly prepared to highlight the natural flavors of the ingredients.

Spondi:

Spondi is a Michelin-starred restaurant in the Pangrati neighborhood, offering a gourmet dining experience. The restaurant's elegant setting and impeccable service set the stage for a culinary journey featuring creative dishes, fine wines, and exquisite desserts. Spondi is a destination for those seeking a sophisticated gastronomic adventure in Athens.

Athens' dining scene is a gastronomic adventure that combines tradition, creativity, and culinary expertise. Whether you're indulging in mezedes at a cozy taverna, savoring fresh seafood by the sea, or experiencing innovative Greek cuisine at a Michelin-starred restaurant, every meal in Athens is a celebration of flavors, culture, and the art of dining.

9.3 STREET FOOD AND LOCAL DELICACIES

Souvlaki:

Souvlaki, grilled meat skewers served in pita bread with vegetables and sauces, is a quintessential Greek street food. Whether it's pork, chicken, or lamb, souvlaki stalls and shops are ubiquitous in Athens. Enjoyed with a side of crispy fries or wrapped in a handheld pita, souvlaki is a flavorful and convenient on-the-go treat.

Koulouri:

Koulouri, a circular bread roll covered in sesame seeds, is a popular street snack in Athens. Often enjoyed as a quick breakfast or snack, koulouri stands can be found throughout the city. Its crunchy exterior and soft interior make it a satisfying and affordable option for a light bite.

Bougatsa:

Bougatsa, a pastry filled with sweet custard, cheese, or minced meat, is a beloved Greek delicacy. In Athens, bakeries and pastry shops serve fresh bougatsa, sprinkled with powdered sugar and cinnamon. This warm and flaky pastry is a delightful indulgence, especially when enjoyed with a strong cup of Greek coffee.

Loukoumades:** Loukoumades are deep-fried dough balls drizzled with honey and sprinkled with cinnamon or powdered sugar. These golden, crispy bites of sweetness are a popular dessert in Athens. Served hot and fresh, loukoumades are a favorite street food indulgence, offering a delightful contrast of textures and flavors.

9.4 VEGETARIAN AND VEGAN OPTIONS:

Vegan Gyros:

In recent years, veganism has gained popularity in Athens, leading to the emergence of vegan-friendly eateries. Vegan gyros, made with plant-based meat alternatives, fresh vegetables, and vegan tzatziki, provide a flavorful and satisfying alternative to the traditional meat-filled version.

Vegetarian Moussaka:

Moussaka, a layered dish with eggplant, potatoes, and a savory tomato-based sauce, is a staple of Greek cuisine. Many restaurants in Athens offer a vegetarian version, omitting the ground meat and incorporating additional vegetables and spices. This hearty and aromatic dish is a favorite among vegetarians and vegans alike.

Vegetarian Souvlaki:

Vegetarian souvlaki, often made with marinated grilled vegetables and tofu or seitan, offers a delicious meat-free alternative. Served in pita bread with fresh salads and sauces, vegetarian souvlaki provides a satisfying and flavorful experience, capturing the essence of the traditional dish without the meat.

9.5 DINING ETIQUETTE:

Tipping: Tipping in Athens is customary and appreciated. A 5-10% tip is considered standard in restaurants. In casual eateries, rounding up the bill is common practice.

Paying the Bill: In Greek restaurants, it's customary for the waiter to bring the bill to the table after the meal. You can pay at the cash register or leave the payment on the table. Credit cards are widely accepted, but it's a good idea to carry some cash for smaller establishments.

Reservations: While it's not always necessary to make reservations, it's advisable for upscale or popular restaurants, especially during the tourist season. Making a reservation ensures you have a table and a smooth dining experience.

Dress Code: Athens is generally casual, but some upscale restaurants may have a smart-casual dress code. It's advisable to check the restaurant's website or contact them in advance if you're unsure about the dress requirements.

Dining in Athens is a delightful experience that caters to a variety of tastes and dietary preferences. Whether you're savoring traditional street food, indulging in vegetarian and vegan delights, or navigating the nuances of dining etiquette, Athens' culinary scene offers a diverse and memorable gastronomic adventure.

10. NIGHTLIFE AND ENTERTAINMENT

10.1 BARS AND NIGHTCLUBS:

Psiri District:

Psiri is a nightlife hub in Athens, teeming with bars, pubs, and nightclubs. Here, you can find everything from trendy cocktail bars to traditional ouzeries. The narrow streets come alive with music, laughter, and the clinking of glasses as locals and tourists mingle in a vibrant atmosphere.

Gazi:

Gazi, once an industrial area, has transformed into a chic nightlife district. The former gasworks buildings now house trendy bars and nightclubs. Gazi is especially popular among the younger crowd, offering an electrifying clubbing scene that lasts until the early morning hours.

Rooftop Bars:

Athens boasts an array of rooftop bars that offer panoramic views of the city and its iconic landmarks, including the Acropolis. These bars, such as A for Athens and 360 Cocktail Bar, provide an elegant ambiance where you can enjoy expertly crafted cocktails while gazing at the illuminated cityscape.

10.2 LIVE MUSIC VENUES:

Half Note Jazz Club:

Half Note Jazz Club, located in Mets, is a legendary venue hosting world-class jazz performances. With its intimate setting and exceptional acoustics, it offers an immersive experience for jazz enthusiasts. The club features both local talents and international jazz artists, creating an atmosphere of musical sophistication.

Rebetadiko:

Rebetadiko, located in Plaka, celebrates rebetiko music, a genre rooted in Greek urban folk music. This venue provides an authentic experience, with live performances of rebetiko songs, traditional instruments, and heartfelt vocals. Visitors can immerse themselves in the soulful melodies and poetic lyrics of this distinctive musical tradition.

10.3 THEATERS AND PERFORMING ARTS:

Herodes Atticus Theater:

This ancient amphitheater, nestled beneath the Acropolis, is a magical venue for live performances. From classical Greek tragedies to contemporary theater productions and concerts, Herodes Atticus Theater offers a unique and enchanting atmosphere, where the arts come to life amidst ancient ruins.

National Theater of Greece:

The National Theater, with its rich history and impressive architecture, stages a variety of theatrical productions, including classic Greek plays, modern dramas, and experimental performances. Attending a play here provides a profound cultural experience, allowing audiences to engage with the nuances of Greek theater.

10.4 CULTURAL NIGHTLIFE EXPERIENCES:

Traditional Tavernas with Live Music:

Many traditional tavernas in areas like Plaka and Psiri feature live music performances, showcasing folk, rebetiko, or traditional Greek tunes. These intimate settings provide an opportunity to savor authentic Greek cuisine while being serenaded by talented musicians, creating a memorable and culturally immersive evening.

Night Tours and Cultural Experiences:

Several tour companies in Athens offer night tours that combine cultural experiences with nightlife. These tours may include visits to archaeological sites under the moonlight, storytelling sessions about ancient myths, and tastings of local wines and delicacies. Such tours provide a unique blend of history, culture, and entertainment, offering a holistic view of Athens' nocturnal charm.

Athens' nightlife and entertainment scene is as diverse as the city itself. Whether you're dancing the night away in a vibrant nightclub, savoring live jazz in an intimate setting, or experiencing the ancient art of Greek theater under the stars, Athens offers an electrifying and culturally enriching nightlife experience that caters to every taste and preference.

11. DAY TRIPS FROM ATHENS

11.1 CAPE SOUNION AND THE TEMPLE OF POSEIDON

Historical Marvel: Cape Sounion, located about 70 kilometers southeast of Athens, is a picturesque headland known for the Temple of Poseidon. This ancient temple, perched atop a cliff overlooking the Aegean Sea, is dedicated to the Greek god of the sea, Poseidon. The site's historical significance and stunning coastal views make it a must-visit destination.

Sunset Magic:

Cape Sounion is particularly renowned for its breathtaking sunsets. As the sun descends over the horizon, casting a golden glow upon the temple and the surrounding sea, visitors are treated to a magical spectacle. Watching the sunset at Cape Sounion is a tranquil and awe-inspiring experience, offering a moment of serenity amidst ancient ruins.

Archaeological Interest:
The Temple of Poseidon is a marvel of ancient Greek architecture. Dating back to the 5th century BCE, the temple's Doric columns and imposing structure exemplify classical Greek design. Exploring the archaeological site provides insight into the religious practices and architectural achievements of ancient Greece, making it a captivating destination for history enthusiasts.

11.2 DELPHI:

Oracle of Delphi:

Delphi, located approximately 180 kilometers northwest of Athens, was once considered the center of the world in ancient Greek religion and mythology. It was home to the Oracle of Delphi, a priestess who was believed to convey prophecies from the god Apollo. The archaeological site of Delphi, nestled on the slopes of Mount Parnassus, includes the Temple of Apollo, the ancient theater, and the Athenian Treasury.

Scenic Splendor

Delphi is surrounded by stunning natural landscapes, with views of olive groves, rugged mountains, and the sparkling waters of the Gulf of Corinth. The site's serene ambiance and the picturesque setting make it a tranquil escape from the bustling city, allowing visitors to immerse themselves in the beauty of the Greek countryside.

Museum of Delphi:

In addition to the archaeological site, Delphi boasts a museum that houses a remarkable collection of artifacts, including sculptures, pottery, and jewelry from ancient times. The museum provides context to the site's historical significance, offering visitors a deeper understanding of the ancient Greek civilization and its cultural achievements.

Sacred Way:

The Sacred Way, the main path leading through the sanctuary of Delphi, was once traversed by pilgrims and visitors. Walking this sacred route allows modern travelers to follow in the footsteps of ancient worshippers, connecting with the spiritual and historical legacy of the site.

Day trips from Athens to Cape Sounion and Delphi offer enriching experiences that blend ancient marvels with natural beauty. Whether you're marveling at the Temple of Poseidon against the backdrop of a golden sunset or exploring the mystical ruins and artifacts of Delphi, these day trips provide a profound connection to Greece's ancient heritage and the timeless allure of its landscapes.

11.3 EPIDAURUS AND MYCENAE

Epidaurus:

Located approximately 120 kilometers from Athens, Epidaurus is renowned for its ancient theater, which is one of the best-preserved in Greece. Built in the 4th century BCE, the theater is an architectural marvel known for its exceptional acoustics. Visitors can stand at the center of the stage and be heard clearly even by the spectators sitting at the highest tiers. The site also includes the Sanctuary of Asclepius, the ancient god of healing, making Epidaurus a testament to ancient Greek medicine and spirituality.

Mycenae:

Mycenae, an archaeological site about 90 kilometers from Athens, was once a powerful center of the Mycenaean civilization. The site features the imposing Lion Gate, the Cyclopean Walls, and the Treasury of Atreus, a monumental tholos tomb. Mycenae's rich history and the mythological connections to figures like King Agamemnon make it a captivating destination for history enthusiasts and admirers of ancient Greek legends.

11.4 HYDRA, POROS, AND AEGINA ISLANDS:

Hydra:

Hydra, one of the Saronic Islands, is a picturesque destination known for its charming harbor, narrow cobblestone streets, and well-preserved neoclassical architecture. Motor vehicles are prohibited on the island, creating a peaceful atmosphere perfect for leisurely strolls. Visitors can explore art galleries, enjoy fresh seafood at seaside tavernas, and relax on Hydra's tranquil beaches.

Poros:

Poros, another gem in the Saronic Gulf, is characterized by lush greenery, crystal-clear waters, and traditional Greek hospitality. The island is adorned with pine forests and citrus orchards, creating a refreshing ambiance. Poros Town, with its neoclassical buildings and waterfront cafes, exudes a relaxed charm. The island's beaches, such as Love Bay and Askeli

Beach, offer ideal spots for sunbathing and swimming.

Aegina:

Aegina, known for its pistachio orchards and ancient temples, is a delightful blend of history and natural beauty. The island's archaeological site includes the Temple of Aphaia, a well-preserved Doric temple dating back to the 5th century BCE. Aegina Town, with its colorful houses and bustling market, is a vibrant hub. Aegina is also famous for its pistachio products, including pistachio ice cream and pastries, offering a delectable culinary experience.

11.5 METEORA MONASTERIES:

Spiritual Marvel: Meteora, a UNESCO World Heritage site located about 350 kilometers from Athens, is a unique collection of monasteries perched atop towering rock formations. These monasteries, originally built in the 14th century, offer breathtaking panoramic views of the surrounding landscape. The monastic community, secluded amid the rock pillars, creates an awe-inspiring and spiritual atmosphere. Visitors can explore some of the monasteries, each with its own history and architectural marvels.

Natural Grandeur: Meteora's geological formations, composed of sandstone and conglomerate rock, are a testament to nature's magnificence. The monasteries, seemingly suspended in mid-air, create a surreal and dramatic spectacle. Exploring the trails and viewpoints around Meteora allows travelers to appreciate the geological wonders and the harmonious integration of human architecture with nature's creations.

These day trips from Athens offer an array of experiences, from immersing in ancient history and archaeological wonders to basking in the serene beauty of Greek islands and witnessing the spiritual grandeur of monastic communities. Each destination provides a unique perspective on Greece's cultural heritage and natural splendor, ensuring a memorable and enriching day trip adventure.

12. OUTDOOR ACTIVITIES

12.1 BEACHES AND WATER SPORTS

Glyfada Beach:

Glyfada, a suburb of Athens, boasts a sandy beach lined with cafes, bars, and water sports facilities. Visitors can indulge in activities like windsurfing, paddleboarding, and jet skiing. The beach's lively atmosphere and crystal-clear waters make it a popular destination for beachgoers and water sports enthusiasts.

Vouliagmeni Beach:

Vouliagmeni, located on the Athenian Riviera, offers a tranquil beach experience surrounded by natural beauty. The beach is known for its thermal springs, providing a unique opportunity for a relaxing soak in warm, mineral-rich waters. Snorkeling, kayaking, and beach volleyball are among the activities enjoyed by visitors here.

12.2 HIKING AND NATURE TRAILS:

Mount Lycabettus:

Rising 300 meters above sea level, Mount Lycabettus offers panoramic views of Athens and the Aegean Sea. Hiking to the summit provides a rewarding experience, especially during sunrise or sunset. The trail is surrounded by pine trees and wildflowers, creating a serene ambiance amidst the bustling city.

Parnitha National Park:

Located just outside Athens, Parnitha National Park offers a network of hiking trails through lush forests, scenic gorges, and alpine meadows. Hikers can explore trails leading to waterfalls, ancient monasteries, and viewpoints with stunning vistas. The park is also home to diverse flora and fauna, making it a haven for nature lovers.

12.3 CYCLING ROUTES:

Athens Bike Tour:

Several companies offer guided bike tours in Athens, allowing cyclists to explore the city's historic sites, neighborhoods, and hidden gems. Cycling along the picturesque coastline and through charming districts like Plaka and Thissio provides a unique perspective of Athens' cultural and architectural heritage.

Sounio Coastal Route:

Cycling along the coastal road from Athens to Cape Sounion offers a scenic journey with views of the Aegean Sea. This route passes through seaside villages, archaeological sites, and pristine beaches. Cyclists can enjoy a refreshing swim at various stops along the way, making it a perfect blend of adventure and relaxation.

12.4 PARKS AND GARDENS:

National Garden of Athens:

Situated in the heart of Athens, the National Garden is an oasis of greenery and tranquility. The garden, adorned with sculptures, ponds, and shaded pathways, offers a serene escape from the urban hustle. It's an ideal spot for picnics, leisurely strolls, and birdwatching amidst the lush flora.

Stavros Niarchos Foundation Cultural Center:

This modern cultural complex includes a large park with gardens, fountains, and a canal. The park hosts events, concerts, and outdoor activities, making it a vibrant hub for both locals and tourists. Visitors can enjoy open-air yoga sessions, art exhibitions, and outdoor movie screenings within this innovative urban space.

12.5 HORSEBACK RIDING:

Kaisariani Riding Club:

Located on the outskirts of Athens, the Kaisariani Riding Club offers horseback riding experiences for riders of all levels. Riding through scenic trails in the foothills of Mount Hymettus, participants can enjoy the natural beauty of the surrounding landscapes. The club also organizes guided rides to archaeological sites, providing a unique blend of history and outdoor adventure.

Athens offers a diverse array of outdoor activities, from beachfront adventures and hiking trails to cycling routes and serene parks. Whether you're seeking adrenaline-pumping water sports, peaceful nature escapes, or cultural explorations on horseback, Athens provides endless opportunities to embrace the great outdoors and experience the city's natural splendor.

13. PRACTICAL INFORMATION

13.1 LANGUAGE AND COMMUNICATION

Language: The official language of Greece is Greek. While many people in Athens, especially in tourist areas, speak English, it's helpful to learn a few basic Greek phrases to enhance your communication and show respect for the local culture.

Communication: Athens has reliable mobile phone coverage and internet connectivity. You can easily obtain a local SIM card or use international roaming services to stay connected. Free Wi-Fi is also available in many cafes, restaurants, and public spaces.

13.2 CURRENCY AND BANKING:

Currency: The official currency of Greece is the Euro (€). ATMs are widely available throughout Athens, allowing you to withdraw cash in Euros. Credit and debit cards are widely accepted in hotels, restaurants, shops, and tourist attractions.

Banking: Banks in Athens typically operate from Monday to Friday, with varying hours. ATMs are available 24/7 and are the most convenient way to access cash. Currency exchange services are offered at banks, exchange bureaus, and some hotels, although ATMs usually offer better rates.

13.3 SAFETY TIPS:

General Safety: Athens is a relatively safe city, but like any major urban area, it's essential to stay vigilant, especially in crowded places. Be aware of pickpockets, particularly in crowded tourist spots and public transportation.

Traffic Safety: Athens can have heavy traffic, so exercise caution when crossing streets. Use pedestrian crossings and obey traffic signals. Greek drivers can be assertive, so be attentive when walking or driving.

Emergency Numbers: The general emergency number in Greece is 112, which connects you to police, fire, ambulance, and other emergency services. For specific emergencies, you can dial 100 for police, 199 for fire, and 166 for medical emergencies.

13.4 LOCAL ETIQUETTE:

Greetings: Greeks are friendly and hospitable people. When meeting someone, a handshake is common. Close friends and family may greet each other with a kiss on both cheeks.

Punctuality: Greeks often have a more relaxed approach to time. While punctuality is appreciated in formal settings, social gatherings might not always start exactly on time.

Tipping: Tipping is customary in Athens. In restaurants, it's common to leave a tip of 5-10% of the total bill. In cafes, rounding up the bill is appreciated. Tipping is also customary for taxi drivers, hotel staff, and tour guides.

13.5 EMERGENCY CONTACTS:

Police: 100
Fire Department: 199
Medical Emergencies: 166
Tourist Police: +30 210 171 3760 (For non-emergency assistance and information)

Athens offers a welcoming environment for travelers. By being aware of the local customs, staying cautious in crowded areas, and knowing the essential emergency contacts, you can make the most of your visit to this historic and vibrant city.

14. TRAVEL TIPS

14.1 PACKING LIST:

Comfortable Footwear:

Athens involves a lot of walking, so bring comfortable walking shoes or sandals. Also, pack a pair of sturdy shoes if you plan on hiking or exploring archaeological sites.

Light Clothing:

Athens has a Mediterranean climate with hot, dry summers. Lightweight and breathable clothing is advisable, along with a hat and sunglasses to protect yourself from the sun.

Modest Attire:

While Athens is cosmopolitan, it's respectful to wear modest clothing when visiting religious sites. For women, carrying a scarf to cover shoulders is a good idea.

Swimwear:

If you plan to visit the beaches, don't forget your swimsuit, sunscreen, and a beach towel.

Travel Adapter:

Greece has Type C and Type F electrical outlets. Make sure to bring the appropriate travel adapter for your electronic devices.

Reusable Water Bottle:

Stay hydrated, especially during hot days. Carry a reusable water bottle and refill it at public fountains, available throughout the city.

Small Backpack:

A small backpack is handy for carrying essentials like water, sunscreen, a map, and your camera during day trips and city explorations.

14.2 BEST TIMES TO VISIT:

Spring (April to June): Spring is one of the best times to visit Athens. The weather is pleasant, and the city's gardens and ancient ruins are in full bloom. It's an ideal time for sightseeing and outdoor activities.

Fall (September to October): Similar to spring, fall offers mild weather and fewer crowds. It's a great time to enjoy the city's attractions comfortably.

Winter (November to February): Athens has a mild winter, making it an excellent destination for travelers seeking a less crowded experience.

While it might rain occasionally, the city's historical and cultural sites are still accessible.

Summer (July to August): Athens can get extremely hot during the summer months, with temperatures often exceeding 30°C (86°F). It's a popular time for tourists, but be prepared for crowded attractions and the need to stay hydrated and cool.

ADDITIONAL TIPS:

Public Transportation Card: Consider getting an Athens Transport Ticket, allowing unlimited travel on public transportation (metro, buses, trams) for a specific duration. It's convenient and saves money if you plan on using public transit frequently.

Local Cuisine: Don't miss the opportunity to indulge in authentic Greek cuisine. Explore local tavernas and try traditional dishes like moussaka, souvlaki, and baklava.

Respect Local Customs: Greeks are proud of their culture and traditions. Respect local customs, especially in religious sites, and learn a few basic Greek phrases to enhance your interactions with locals.

Travel Insurance: It's always advisable to have travel insurance that covers medical emergencies, trip cancellations, and unexpected events.

By keeping these travel tips in mind, you can enhance your experience in Athens, ensuring a smooth and enjoyable journey in this historic city.

14.3 BUDGETING AND COSTS

Accommodation: Athens offers a range of accommodation options, from budget hostels to luxurious hotels. Consider staying in areas like Psiri or Monastiraki, which are central and have various budget-friendly choices.

Dining: Dining in Athens can be affordable, especially if you explore local eateries and tavernas. Look for places frequented by locals for authentic and budget-friendly meals. Souvlaki stands and bakeries offer tasty and inexpensive options.

Transportation: Public transportation in Athens is relatively cheap and efficient. Consider getting an Athens Transport Ticket for unlimited rides on buses, trams, and the metro. Taxis are also reasonably priced compared to many other European cities.

Attractions: Many archaeological sites and museums offer reduced or free admission for students and EU citizens under 25. Plan your visits accordingly to save on entrance fees. Additionally, some sites have free admission days, so check in advance.

14.4 VISA AND ENTRY REQUIREMENTS:

Visa: Greece is a Schengen Area country. Depending on your nationality, you might need a Schengen Visa to enter Greece. Check the official Greek consulate or embassy website to confirm visa requirements for your country of residence.

EU and EEA Citizens: Citizens of European Union (EU) and European Economic Area (EEA) countries do not need a visa to enter Greece. They can stay for up to 90 days within a 180-day period.

Passport Validity: Ensure your passport is valid for at least three months beyond your planned date of departure from Greece.

14.5 USEFUL APPS AND RESOURCES:

Visit Greece App: The official tourism app provides information about attractions, events, dining, and accommodation. It works offline, making it convenient for travelers without continuous internet access.

Google Maps: A reliable tool for navigating Athens. It offers directions for walking, driving, and public transportation, helping you plan your routes effectively.

Athens Metro and Bus App: This app provides real-time information about Athens' metro and bus schedules. It's useful for planning your public transportation journeys on the go.

XE Currency Converter: A handy app for converting currencies, allowing you to keep track of expenses and understand prices in your home currency.

TripAdvisor: A valuable resource for finding restaurants, accommodations, and attractions. Read reviews and recommendations from fellow travelers to enhance your Athens experience.

By considering these practical tips, you can make the most of your visit to Athens, ensuring a memorable and enjoyable exploration of this ancient city.

15.0 CONCLUSION

15.1 SUMMARY OF KEY POINTS:

In this comprehensive Athens travel guide, we've explored the captivating facets of the ancient city, offering detailed insights into its historical marvels, cultural richness, and contemporary allure. Here's a summary of the key points:

Historical Marvels: Athens stands as a testament to ancient Greece, boasting iconic landmarks such as the Acropolis, Parthenon, and Ancient Agora. Exploring these sites provides a deep dive into the city's historical significance.

Cultural Experiences: From museums and art galleries to traditional festivals and Greek plays, Athens offers a vibrant cultural scene. Delving into Greek cuisine, music, and dance enhances the cultural immersion.

Outdoor Activities: Nature enthusiasts can indulge in beach activities, hiking, cycling, and horseback riding, exploring both the urban and natural landscapes of Athens.

Practical Information: Essential travel tips include language and communication nuances, currency details, safety tips, local etiquette, emergency contacts, and insights into visa requirements. Knowing these practicalities ensures a smooth and enjoyable trip.

Day Trips: Athens' proximity to destinations like Cape Sounion, Delphi, and the islands of Hydra, Poros, and Aegina offers travelers enriching day trip opportunities, combining ancient history, scenic beauty, and island charms.

15.2 FINAL THOUGHTS:

Athens, with its blend of ancient grandeur and modern vitality, is a city that mesmerizes every traveler. Its archaeological wonders speak of a rich historical legacy, while its lively neighborhoods, delectable cuisine, and vibrant cultural scene showcase the city's dynamic spirit. Whether you're exploring the Acropolis under the Athenian sun, savoring souvlaki in a bustling market, or witnessing a sunset over Cape Sounion, Athens leaves an indelible mark on the soul.

In Athens, history breathes, culture dances, and the warmth of the people welcomes you like an old friend. It's not just a city; it's an experience that immerses you in the heart of ancient Greece while embracing the contemporary rhythm of a bustling metropolis. As you wander through its historic streets and modern avenues, Athens whispers tales of gods and philosophers, inviting you to be a part of its timeless narrative.

So, pack your bags, learn a few Greek phrases, and embark on a journey to Athens. Let the city's ancient stones and modern energy guide you, and in return, you'll discover a destination that will forever hold a piece of your traveler's heart.

Safe travels and may your Athenian adventure be filled with unforgettable moments and everlasting memories. Opa!

Printed in Poland
by Amazon Fulfillment
Poland Sp. z o.o., Wrocław